Di

Space!

Peter Patrick

William Thomas

What happens on the mission, stays on the mission...

Diary of a Super Spy: Space!

(Diary of a Sixth Grade Super Spy: Book 4)

Peter Patrick, William Thomas

For Ethan, Chelsea, and Sophie.

Also in the Diary of a Super Spy series:

Diary of a Super Spy

Attack of the Ninjas!

A Giant Problem!

Evil Attack!

Daylight Robbery!

Pirates!

Diary of a Super Spy:

Space!

Peter Patrick

William Thomas

Chapter 1

Math Class

Another math test…

I bet teachers lie in bed at night and dream up new ways to torture their students. This time, Mrs. Jackson has developed the ultimate torture – a ten-page math test on everything we have studied this year.

Oh man…

My name is Charlie Chucky, I am in the sixth grade, I love playing Minecraft, and I am learning to become a Super Spy.

My Dad is the world's best Super Spy, and he is starting to teach me all his tricks. Lately, I've been battling invisible giants, crazy zombie teachers, and super ninjas!

Life has been pretty crazy, and I've enjoyed every second of it.

My best friend Harley is different to me. He doesn't want to become a Super Spy. He doesn't want to battle bad guys and save the world each week. Nope. He wants to sit indoors and stare at numbers all day. Harley's dream is to become the world's greatest math professor.

He loves school, he loves studying, and he absolutely *loves* math tests.

He goes mad for them. It is the one thing he is *really* good at.

He just loves numbers.

Numbers are like candy for him – he can't get enough of it. He even asked Mrs. Jackson for extra math homework last night. Mrs. Jackson then decided to give the whole class extra math homework.

Let's just say Harley wasn't that popular after school.

This is Harley.

Mrs. Jackson always says that someday math will save our lives, but I can't see how it will.

Maybe one day, four giant numbers will attack our school, and I will defeat them using an algebra equation... or maybe the numbers in my textbook will go bad, and start attacking all the words on the pages, and I will stop them using a calculator!

Maybe.

Or maybe not.

About halfway through the math test, I lose concentration and stare out the window, dreaming about all the crazy things I get to do. I wonder what I will get to do today? Maybe I'll battle chocolate frogs, or an ice-cream monster. That way, I could defeat them by eating them for dessert. Hmmm... they would be the best bad guys ever.

As I stare out the window at a cloud that looks like a giant hotdog riding a toy elephant, I see something in the sky.

It looks like some sort of spaceship.

And it is falling.

Fast.

Really, really fast!

That is so cool!

A spaceship! Or a UFO! Or a flying saucer! Or a space cup!

Whatever you want to call it, it is cool!

But...

CRASH!

Whatever has fallen from the sky has crashed into the ground at a really fast pace!

That looks totally dangerous.

Wait a minute...

It looks like it has crashed right next to my house!

Chapter 2

The Crash Landing

After the bell rings to end the school day, I throw my half-completed math test at Mrs. Jackson, and then race out the door to get to my house.

"How much fun was that math test?!" Harley yells in excitement as he follows me.

"It wasn't fun at all!" I yell back.

"I loved it! I really loved question 10. What a great question! You know, the one about-"

"It was torture, Harley! How could you find a test about numbers fun? Math will never be useful in real life! Teachers only make us do it so they can torment us!"

"I thought it was fun. I asked Mrs. Jackson for an extra copy so I can do it again on the weekend," Harley sighs. "Hey, why are you running?"

"When I was looking out the window during the math test, I saw something fall from the sky into my backyard, and I want to know what it is. Now, keep up!"

"Looking out the window?" Harley is running beside me now. "When did you have time to look out the window? I was too busy doing my math test, and then checking my answers twice. I even wrote some math questions for Mrs. Jackson on the last page. She loves it when I do that. Last time I did it, she called me a 'smarty pants.' She thinks I am so clever that even my pants are smart! I think she really likes me."

"Um, ok," I roll my eyes. "Just keep up."

Harley and I race all the way back to my house, sprinting down the street to see what happened.

When we arrive, we dash into the yard to see what has crashed. My Super Spy Dad is already studying it.

"Cool!" Harley yells.

But Dad looks worried.

Very worried.

"What is it?" I ask Dad.

"What sort of question is that, Charlie?" Dad looks at me. "It's clearly a spaceship."

"What's a spaceship doing in our backyard?"

"I was trying to fly it by remote control, but it flew out of range. That's why it has crashed in our backyard. It tracked the original signal back to the location of the tracker. We have designed all our Super Spy spaceships to behave like that. But I didn't want it to come back here."

"It doesn't even look damaged?" Harley says.

"Yes, Harley," Dad says as he kicks the side of the spaceship. "All our spaceships are designed to be extra cushiony, so if they crash, they are not damaged by the impact."

"But why were you trying to fly a spaceship?" Harley questions.

"Because there's a giant meteor heading towards Earth that will crush us all into tiny little pieces if it isn't stopped," Dad says calmly.

"A meteor?!" Harley begins to panic. "Coming to Earth?! Our Earth? But I don't want to die. There is so much I haven't done yet – like learn Modularity Theorem!"

"What is Modularity Theorem?" I ask.

"The theorem states that any elliptic curve over Q can be obtained via a rational map with integer coefficients from the classical modular curve $X_0(N)$ for integer N and is a curve with integer coefficients with an explicit definition. If N is the smallest integer for which the parameterization can be sourced, then it may be defined in terms of mapping generated by a particular kind of modular form of weight two and level N! This, of course, is an integer q-expansion, and can be followed by an isogeny. Der! How could you not know that, Charlie?"

"Um, yep. Sure, Harley. I totally knew that. The old Modularity Theorem. I am totally all over that theorem. I studied that theorem along with the, um, er... The Star Wars Theorem. You know, the one where $r2 = d2$ and $dd = ee$, and $qq = 56$," I reply, trying to sound smart. I made up that last theorem. I think Harley knows that.

"There is no Star Wars Theorem in math, Charlie. But Modularity Theorem is widely regarded as the hardest math theorem in history! And if a meteor crashes into Earth, then I will never get to learn it! I must go home now, and start studying it!"

"Calm down," I grab Harley by the arms. "A meteor isn't going to crash into Earth. My Dad wouldn't let that happen. And nobody is going to die. You'll have plenty of time to read your precious mathematic books and study the theorems of models and catwalks."

"I wouldn't be so sure of that, Charlie," Dad mumbles as he looks at the spaceship. "We have been trying to stop this meteor for months, but nothing has worked. We've sent up rockets, explosives, dinosaurs, and tracking missiles. Nothing has stopped that meteor racing towards our planet. Everything we send up there just comes back to Earth. This ship was our final hope of stopping the meteor crashing into us. There is nothing to stop it now."

"Why don't you just blast the meteor out of the sky? You could use one of those mega-powerful rockets to smash it to pieces. That would be easy."

"We have tried that, Charlie, but there is a major problem. The meteor appears to have a force-field around the outside protecting it from any attack we make. Nothing we have sent up there has been able to break through the barrier of that force-field."

"A force-field? Is that normal for a meteor?" Harley asks. "That seems quite strange. I haven't learned about force-fields on meteors at school."

"It isn't normal," Dad replies. "Meteors don't usually have force-fields. What it means is that someone is protecting the meteor. It is likely that the force-field is being generated by a piece of equipment on the surface of the meteor. We don't know why."

"Do you know X?" Harley attempts to make a math joke.

"No," Dad replies, not getting the joke about x and y. "We invented this special spaceship for situations exactly like this. This spaceship has been specifically designed to break through any force-field that exists. If we were able to break through the force-field, then we could blast the meteor out of the sky."

"Then what's the problem?"

"The range is too far for the remote control of this spaceship. This spaceship can only travel a short distance via remote control before the signal is lost. We would have to wait until the meteor is very close to Earth, and by then, it would be too late."

"So why don't you just climb into the spaceship and fly up there?" Harley asks.

"Because this is only a prototype spaceship, Harley. It was designed to be an experimental spaceship before we built the real one. However, we don't have enough time to complete the real one. If we don't stop that meteor, then it will hit Earth tomorrow!"

"That's bad," Harley comments.

"It's just too small! Look, I don't fit! I can't fly it into outer space if I can't fit inside!" Dad attempts to climb inside the small spaceship.

"But it's not just about the force-field," Dad adds. "We have encountered this sort of dilemma before. On the other side of the force-field is likely to be two alien guards defending the force-field generator machine."

"Alien guards?"

"Yes, Charlie. Alien guards. They are like normal guards, but they are alien. We had this issue back in 1963, but we negotiated with the guards, and they agreed to turn the meteor around if we donated trousers to them."

"Trousers?" Harley asks.

"Yes, Harley. Trousers. You know, like pants."

"Oh, right. Why did they want trousers?"

"I have no idea, Harley. In 1963, we sent our best Super Spy to the meteor, and she negotiated a deal with them. We haven't seen a large meteor like this since."

"Alien guards defending a force-field machine on a speeding meteor? Wow. That's well crazy, Dad," I say.

"Yes, Charlie. It is crazy."

"What are we going to do?"

"We need someone to fly the spaceship through the force-field, defeat the alien guards, turn off the force-field generator machine, and steer the meteor away from Earth."

"How would you steer it away from Earth?" Harley asks.

"This steering control panel will allow us to steer the meteor any direction we want," Dad holds up a small machine. "But it won't work if the force-field is on. We need to find someone small enough to fly this spaceship, travel up to the meteor, and turn off the force-field first. We need someone about half the size of an adult human, someone who is able to fit inside this spaceship..."

Then Dad looks at Harley and I.

Here we go...

Chapter 3

The Spaceship

"I'll do it!" I jump at the chance to fly into outer space.

Ever since I first looked at the stars and realized that they are enormous, bright spheres of very hot plasma gas radiating energy from the process of nuclear fusion by burning hydrogen to make helium, I've always wanted to go into space.

"Sorry Charlie, but this small spaceship requires two people to fly it," Dad says. "You can't fly this spaceship alone. You will need another volunteer before you can fly it."

"Harley will come too!" I volunteer Harley to come with me.

Harley isn't the bravest boy going around.

He would much rather sit at home, play computer games, and read math textbooks.

Spiders on the television usually scare him.

Last time he saw a spider in real life, he froze in shock. It was two days before he moved again.

"Harley," Dad looks over to him. "Do you agree that you will fly into outer space, risking your life to save the Earth?"

"Um-"

"Yes!" I interrupt him before he can refuse. "Harley would love to do it! He loves to do really, really dangerous things! He would love to come with me into space!"

"Um-" Harley mumbles.

"Then it's a done deal," Dad says. "It is up to the two of you to stop that massive meteor crashing into Earth. I have faith that you can complete this very dangerous, risky, treacherous, and hazardous journey. I am proud of you boys for agreeing to risk your lives to save Earth."

"But I don't-" Harley tries to argue with us.

"There is no time to waste!" Dad says. "We are running out of time, and we need you to stop that meteor. It is due to crash into Earth tomorrow morning, so you have to move now. Hop in."

Dad throws a spacesuit into our hands and pushes us towards the spaceship.

"But I don't-" Harley continues to protest.

"There is no time for that nonsense," Dad interrupts Harley. "You're the Earth's last line of defense against this meteor. You must fly up to the meteor, go through the force-field, defeat the alien guards, turn off the force-field generator machine, and then turn that meteor around! You can do it!"

"But I-" Harley says.

"If you don't stop that meteor, then nobody will be here to teach you math," Dad convinces Harley to go. "You must hurry!"

Dad pushes hard as he squeezes Harley and I into the tiny spaceship.

"There are certain things that I need to tell you about directing this spaceship. Firstly, do not open the doors of the spaceship until you have landed. That is important. And before you land, you must press the red colored button, followed by the auburn colored button, followed by the scarlet colored button, followed by the crimson colored button, followed by the rose colored button, and then the red colored button again. Do not get the order of those buttons wrong. If you do not press the buttons in that order, you will smash heavily when you land. The spaceship is crash-proof, which means that it will bounce rather than crash, but it will still hurt if you don't get the landing right."

"Um, ok," I look at the buttons on the spaceship, but they all look like the same color red to me. "Sure thing, Dad. No worries."

"And you must only squeeze the particle accelerator motion switch when you are exactly 114.63 miles from the meteor. If you press the switch any later, you will not land safely. If you press it any earlier, you will miss the meteor. Once the particle accelerator motion switch has been activated, you must desensitize the spaceship by initiating the triple-double-quad water sprinkler. If this is done accurately, then you will land safely. If you get this wrong, your landing will be very dangerous."

"Sure, Dad," I reply. I look over to Harley, hoping that he is taking notes about how to fly the spaceship, but he is busy adjusting his helmet.

"And when you land, you must find the force-field generator machine, turn it off, and put this steering control panel in the middle of the meteor. You must then activate it by rubbing the side electronic panel using only your middle finger."

"What does the steering control panel do?" I ask.

"This will give us control over the meteor. By using the magnetic force of the machine, we will be able to steer the meteor away from Earth, but it won't work with the force-field still on. The force-field interrupts any signal that we send. Now, you'd better hurry, Charlie – we are running out of time. You must go now."

"What did your Dad just say?" Harley asks me. "I couldn't hear him because I was putting my helmet on correctly."

"Oh, he didn't say anything important," I shrug. "Just that we have to push the red button, followed by a switch, and then turn on the sprinklers for our yard. Nothing essential."

"Ok," Harley shrugs. "So how do we steer this thing?"

"Oh, right. Yes," Dad replies. "You must control the spaceship using the gamer control pad. When we were building the prototype for the spaceship, it was the only thing left in the room, so we designed the ship to move with the commands of the gamer control pad."

"Uh?" I question. "I don't know how to use that control pad."

"It's alright, Charlie," Harley smiles. "I've played a computer game that used the same controls. You need to move the controls like this."

Harley punches a lot of buttons, leans the controls forwards, kisses the game pad, and then suddenly...

BOOM!

We have launched into the air!

The spaceship has taken off!

I hold on tight as the spaceship wobbles and shakes.

"Harley, fly this thing in a straight line!"

"Hang on," Harley calls out. He hits a few buttons, twirls the joystick, and then punches the gamer control pad. "There!"

Suddenly, we are flying in a straight line towards the sky!

"Great job, Harley!" I yell as we race through the clouds.

Woo-hoo!

Space – here we come!

Chapter 4

Space!

After rocketing out of the Earth's atmosphere, we fly into outer space and soar towards the meteor.

This is *so* super cool!

We are in outer space!

Flying into space is so awesome – it's everything I thought it would be. I can see so many stars, and planets, and the moon looks so much bigger up here.

"Hey, Harley, look!" I point back towards Earth as we leave the atmosphere. "If you look back there, you can see the North Pole! The Earth looks so awesome from up here."

But Harley doesn't say anything – he is afraid of heights.

"There's nothing to be scared of, Harley," I say, trying to calm him down.

"But we are so far up," he quivers. "You know that I am no good with heights. We are so high!"

"No, we're not," I say. "It's not like you can fall out here. If you fall out of the spaceship, then you won't fall very far, because there is no gravity. You won't fall back to Earth. You'll just float along in the nothingness forever, never actually getting anywhere. See? Nothing to be afraid of at all."

Harley doesn't respond.

I don't think that helped.

We continue the trip into space, and I try to remember what my Dad told me about the red buttons... I can't remember what he said, so I just hit all the buttons at once.

I don't think that's a great idea, but it is going to have to do.

As we head towards the force-field, I hope that we are able to drive through it...

Woo!

We fly straight through the force-field that is surrounding the meteor.

"We'll land on that flat section over there," I say. "I just need to try to remember what Dad said about landing… he said 'Hit a switch, and then hit a red button, and turn on the tap'… I think that is what he said."

Harley doesn't respond. He is gripping the edges of the spaceship tightly as we approach the meteor.

"Um, Charlie," Harley shakes. "We seem to be approaching the landing much too fast. If we continue at this speed, we are going to crash…"

"Don't worry about it," I smile. "Dad said that this spaceship is designed to withstand crash landings. We'll be fine."

"I don't want to crash, Charlie!"

"No problem! I just have to push this red button, followed by this switch…"

"Charlie!" Harley sounds really nervous. "We are going too fast to land on the meteor! We are going to crash!"

"It's alright," I say calmly. "I just have to punch this switch, and turn this dial…"

"Charlie! We have to slow down!"

"It's ok," I say as I press every button on the control panel.

"Charlie!"

Um, yep.

Maybe Harley is right.

We do seem to be going to fast to land safely on the meteor...

SLAM!

We crash into the meteor!

Luckily, the spaceship bounces – first on the wing, then on the nose, and then on the back.

We bounce four times before coming to a stop in front of a big rock.

Ouch.

"Hashtag Rough Landing," I say, as I open the doors of the spaceship and climb out. "I really should have listened to what Dad had to say about the controls. That way we could have landed a lot easier."

After climbing out of the tiny spaceship, I shake my body, dust myself off, and begin to walk around the meteor.

This place is amazing.

It is just like the moon – it's covered in space rocks and dust, and I can even see Earth off in the distance. Planet Earth looks like a little star. That is so awesome.

I wonder if aliens sing songs about Earth – 'Twinkle, twinkle, little Earth…'

"Hey Harley, you should see this… Harley? Harley? Where are you? Are you ok?"

I turn around, but I can't find Harley.

Where is he?

Running back to the spaceship, I call out to Harley again. "Harley? Harley? Where are you? Are you hurt?"

"I'm not here," I hear a muffled noise from inside the ship. "There is no-one named Harley here. Go away."

Harley is hiding in the spaceship, scared of what is out here.

"Come on, Harley. We are in space! This is amazing! You have to check out the view of planet Earth! It looks so tiny! Although, I'm sure if you look hard enough, you would still be able to see Mr. Hazel's nose."

Our language teacher, Mr. Hazel, has a big nose. When he sneezes, the entire room shakes.

"No. I don't want to come out of the spaceship, Charlie," Harley's voice shakes as he talks. "It's safe in here. I've done my bit – I flew the spaceship into space. Now, you go and save the world. I'll wait here for you."

"Come on, Harley! This is one of the greatest moments of our lives. This might be the only chance you get in your whole life to dance on a meteor! This is so cool, Harley," I start dancing on the meteor. I would do the moonwalk, but as this isn't the moon, I don't think that would be appropriate.

"No, Charlie. Not this time. It's too dangerous. Maybe next time we come into space, I will be the first person to dab in space, but not today. Today, I am staying inside this spaceship."

"Harley! We. Are. In. Space! You've got to walk around and check this out! Anyway, I need your help to locate the force-field generator. Remember, we still have to save the world."

"Hmph," Harley begins to slowly climb out of the spaceship and puts his foot nervously on the meteor. "I'm here to find that force-field generator machine, turn it off, put down the steering control panel, and then we're out of here. I'm not spending an extra second longer here than I have to. If you promise that you won't play around, then I will help you. Promise?"

"Fine," I reply. "I won't play around. I will just look for the force-field generator machine."

Harley reaches back into the spaceship and collects the steering control panel that will help steer the meteor once the force-field has been turned off. He places the steering control panel on a flat piece of meteor-rock, and turns it on.

"Right. The steering control panel is on," Harley says. "Now all we have to do is find the force-field machine, and turn it off. Simple, right?"

"Sure is," I smile. "You go that way, and I will go this way."

Harley and I start to walk in different directions, looking for the force-field generator machine. It's hard to look for something when you don't even know what it looks like. For all I know, this rock could be a force-field machine.

Or this rock.

Or that rock.

There are a lot of rocks on a meteor, and not much else.

"There it is! Charlie, I've found it!" Harley yells. "Over here! I've found the force-field generator machine! It looks just like a toaster!"

I race over to join Harley, who is staring at the machine.

He's right. It does look just like a toaster.

"Are you sure that's it?" I question.

"Of course," Harley replies. "Look. You can see the rays of the force-field coming out from the top of the machine. And there doesn't appear to be anything else on this meteor. That has to be it!"

"I suppose you're right," I reply.

"Great! Let's go turn it off!" Harley starts to run towards the machine. "All we have to do is switch it off, and then we can go home! I'm going over there, Charlie! This is too easy! We should come into space more often. There is nothing to be afraid of at all!"

"Harley! Wait! We haven't found the alien guards yet!" I try to stop him. "Wait! Harley!"

"There are no other life forms around here," Harley bravely runs towards the machine. "It's just us, space, and the machine. Nothing to worry about, Charlie! Let's do it!"

"Harley! Wait!" I yell again, but he keeps running. "Wait!"

And then…

WHACK!

Chapter 5

The Alien Guards

Harley goes flying across the meteor!

What happened?!

I look behind Harley, and see an alien guard standing there!

Agh!

Harley was hit by the alien guard!

"Harley! Harley! Are you ok?" I shout as I run to help my friend. "Harley!"

"It's ok, Charlie. I'm fine," Harley groans as he rubs his helmet. "What hit me?"

"Look," I say quietly, pointing towards the alien walking towards us.

Oh no...

The alien doesn't look happy.

Actually, he could be happy. I'm not sure what happy aliens look like. They might even frown when they are happy.

The alien that walks towards us has big round eyes, antennas, a long stomach, a belt, and he is wearing trousers around his ankles. Weird.

"What is that?" Harley's voice shakes as he hides behind me. "Charlie, we need to get out of here. Fast."

"Don't worry, Harley," I reply. "I'm sure the alien is nice. He's probably really friendly. We'll just explain to him what we are doing here and then ask him nicely to turn the meteor around. There is nothing to worry about at all, Harley. We've got this."

The alien walks towards us, arms out wide, staring at us with anger.

Maybe he doesn't look so friendly...

"Get off our meteor!" the alien guard states firmly. "You need to go home. This is our meteor, and we do not want visitors! Go home!"

"Hello," I greet the alien. "My name is Charlie, and this is my friend Harley. We are from the planet Earth, which you can see in the distance over there. We have come to your meteor to ask you to turn it around and go home."

"No," the alien replies.

"Please?"

"No."

"Pretty please?"

"No.

"Pretty please with a cherry on top?"

"The answer is still no."

Well, that's all I've got. I don't know what to do now!

The giant alien's arm goes backward, and he gets ready to hit me!

"Wait!" I stop him. "Before you hit me, you need to tell me who you are. I deserve to know which alien is about to hit me."

"You know who we are!" the alien yells.

"Um… nope. Sorry. I've got nothing. I have no idea who you are."

"Yes, you do."

"No, I don't."

"Yes, you do."

"Sorry, Mister. I have no idea who you are. I have never seen you before."

"Yes. You do know who we are. We are famous! Look at us! You must know who we are!" the alien announces as a second alien guard walks towards us.

"Um… nope. Still nothing."

"We are the Trouserdown Guards!" the alien announces.

"The trouser down guards?" I question, looking at the trousers around his ankles.

"No. I said the Trouserdown Guards."

"The trouser down guards?"

"Nooo… the Trouserdown Guards."

"Oh… the trouser down guards."

"No," he replies slowly. "We are the Trouserdown Guards. It is one word, not two. Trouserdown, not trouser down."

"Oh… right. The good old Trouserdown Guards," I pretend to know who they are.

"We sent Earth a video last month saying that we want all of your trousers to be delivered to our planet, or will we attack Earth with a giant meteor! We were very clear in the video."

"A video? How did you send it?"

"We sent the video via intergalactic email."

"Nope. Sorry. We mustn't have got it. Do you mind resending it, and giving us another week before you hit us with the giant meteor?"

"Oh, ok," the alien replies, looking confused. "No worries. We will go back home, and resend the intergalactic email to Earth."

I turn around, and start walking back to our spaceship.

Well, that was easy.

"No! Wait!" the second alien guard yells. "We have already given you a week. That is long enough. It is time for you to deliver all of your trousers! We will not give you any more time!"

"Yeah! Delivery time!" the dumb one says. "Now is the time for delivery! That's why we call it delivery time!"

"So you want all the trousers on Earth, or you will crash this meteor into our planet?" I ask.

"That's right! We have no more trousers left. We need a new supply. Without trousers, our ankles will get very cold. We are from a very cold planet, and we do not like having cold ankles. And you can see by the size of our big hands, we cannot sew new pairs of trousers ourselves. That's why we need yours. We asked nicely, but nobody responded to us. Now it is time to take action!"

"Ok, ok," I try to calm the guards down. "Let us go back to our spaceship and call Earth to see what we can do. We will ask nicely, and I am sure that they will send all the trousers to you very quickly. There is no need to worry about anything. We will get this sorted out."

"No. You will stay with us until we crash into your planet. We will not allow you to return to your spaceship."

"Why not?" I question.

"Because you might try to stop us. And if you know anything, then you must know that the Trouserdown Guards will not be defeated! We are un-defeatablely."

"That's not even a word," Harley calls out from over my shoulder. "You can't just start making up words!"

"It is a word on our planet!" the second Trouserdown Guard replies. "And so is squashie-squashie."

"What does that mean?"

"It is when we sit on something, and we flatten it. And that is what we are going to do to you! Squashie-squashie! Squashie-squashie!"

Oh no.

I turn to Harley and whisper, "I have a plan. On the count of three, run back to the spaceship. We need to call Dad to get help. He will know what to do."

"What? I can't run. You know I'm not a fast runner," Harley whispers back.

"Harley, we don't have a choice…"

"One..."

"Two..."

"Three! Run!"

We start to run away from the alien guards, but the lack of gravity on the meteor means that we float when we run.

That's not good!

The Trouserdown Guards are going to catch us!

I look over my shoulder to see how close they are...

But the problem with wearing trousers around your ankles is that you can't run very fast...

Chapter 6

Calling Earth

Harley and I race back to the spaceship, leaving the Trouserdown Guards tripping behind us.

Harley jumps straight into the driver's seat of the spaceship, and starts playing with the controls.

"Harley, where are you going?" I ask. "We can't leave now! The force-field is still on! We have to get to the force-field generator machine and turn it off!"

"No way. We're going home, Charlie. We can't defeat aliens that size. We have no chance against the Trouserdown Guards! Did you see how big they are? And they are aliens! Big aliens! That is not what I signed up for."

"We can't go home, Harley. We have to turn off the force-field generator machine and stop the meteor crashing into Earth. It is up to us to save the world. There isn't enough time to go back to Earth."

Harley looks at me with questioning eyes. He knows I'm right.

Reluctantly, he hands me the Intergalactic Communicator to call my Dad at Super Spy Headquarters.

"Dad!" I yell into the transmitter device.

"Charlie. I'm at Super Spy Headquarters, and we have been monitoring your progress. Tell us what you have found on the meteor."

"Dad, we've planted the steering control panel on the meteor, but there are alien guards here! They are blocking us from turning off the force-field generator machine. And they are not friendly alien guards – they are huge!"

"We need that force-field turned off, Charlie. The fate of planet Earth rests on you and Harley completing the mission. If the force-field is still on, we can't steer the meteor away. You must turn it off!"

"But the guards are too big!" I reply.

"Who are the alien guards, Charlie? What are their names?"

"The Trouserdown Guards."

"The trouser down guards? Never heard of them."

"No, Dad. I said the Trouserdown Guards, not the trouser down guards. It's one word, not two."

"Oh... the Trouserdown Guards. Yes. I have heard of them before. They come from the planet Green Cold Peppers."

"Um… I've never heard of that planet, Dad. It's not in any of my school text books."

"No, son. It wouldn't be. I traveled there by mistake via a teleporter many, many years ago. The planet is located many galaxies away from Earth."

"Really?"

"Oh yes, Charlie. The natives of that planet were nice aliens. Probably the nicest aliens I've come across. A lot nicer than the Trouser-up aliens. The Trouser-up aliens were not nice at all."

"What else do you know about the Trouserdown Guards? Is there anything that you know that might help us?"

"The Trouserdown Guards were also the same aliens that drove the meteor here in 1963, when one of the agency's spies stopped them."

"Well, they're back, Dad! And they aren't being very nice!"

"I gave them a present when I left their planet last time… let me think what that was…"

"We don't have time for you to reminisce about your past, Dad. We are on a meteor heading straight for Earth, remember? We have to figure out a way to defeat the huge alien guards, or we can't stop the meteor."

"Oh yes… I remember now. I gave them 2000 pairs of extra-extra large trousers and 320,000 pairs of extra-extra large socks."

"Why?"

"Because it is very cold on their planet, and their hands are to big to sew their own clothes. But they only get cold ankles. The rest of their bodies don't feel the cold, it is just their ankles. So they wore the trousers around their ankles to keep them warm."

"Great story Dad, but what do we do about this meteor? It has a force-field around it, remember?"

"Yes... Charlie, I have a plan that may help you. One of you will have to distract the Trouserdown Guards while the other turns off the force-field. Then we can steer the meteor away from Earth using the magnetic force of the steering control panel."

"If we get to the force-field generator machine, how do we turn it off? Is there an off-switch?"

"There is no off-switch, Charlie. You will need to find the red wire on the force-field generator machine, and cut it. That will disrupt the electromagnetic fields from the generator and force it to self-destruct."

"Got it."

"And Charlie..."

"Yes, Dad?"

"Be careful. Those Trouserdown Guards might be dumb, but they are very, very strong."

"Got it, Dad. I will call you again once the force-field generator machine has been turned off."

"Good luck, Charlie."

Hanging up the Intergalactic Communicator, I look over to Harley.

"We are not going home yet, are we?" Harley asks.

"No, Harley," I shake my head. "We have to save planet Earth."

"But how, Charlie? How can we possibly defeat those aliens?"

I place my hand on Harley's shoulder, "The Trouserdown Guards are dumb. We know that. We will have to distract them long enough to turn off the force-field generator machine. Once we have done that, we can go home."

Harley looks down to the ground.

"Why did I follow Charlie home today?" he whispers to himself. "I knew this was going to end badly. I should have just gone home and read more math text books."

"Harley, you will need to distract the Trouserdown Guards while I try to turn off the force-field generator. Dad explained to me how to turn it off."

"But-"

"There is no time to think, Harley. This isn't a math test. We have to go and save planet Earth!"

Chapter 7

Saving Earth...

"Hi," Harley quivers as he walks up to the alien guards.

The alien guards stare at Harley. They look like they want to tear him apart.

"Before you hit me, I want to know if you have heard the joke about the trousers?" Harley asks.

"Joke? No, we haven't heard the joke about the trousers. We do not tell jokes on our planet. It is too cold for jokes, but we like jokes. They make us laugh," the Trouserdown Guards reply. "Tell us the joke."

"Um… ok. Now, I just have to remember the punchline…"

"Tell us!" the alien guard yells. "Tell us the joke!"

"Ok. Ok. Um… did you hear the joke about the alien with five legs?"

"No. We have not heard this joke."

"The trousers fitted like a glove!" Harley laughs.

"Hahahaha!" one alien guard laughs.

"I don't get it," the dumb one says. "I do not understand the comedy in the joke."

"Gloves have five fingers, so when you put trousers on an alien with five legs, they fit like a glove," Harley explains.

"Oh, ok," the Trouserdown Guard nods. "Tell us the joke again."

"The same joke?" Harley questions. "I have other jokes I can tell you."

"No! I want to hear the same joke!"

"Um, sure," Harley shrugs. "Did you hear about the alien with five legs?"

"Yes! His trousers fitted like a glove! Hahahaha!" the Trouserdown Guards fall to the ground laughing together. "Hahahaha!"

The alien guards are definitely distracted now.

Also, this is probably the first time anyone has ever laughed at Harley's very bad jokes.

As Harley keeps the alien guards distracted, I sneak around the back of them and find the force-field generator machine.

"That was a very good joke," one of the Trouserdown Guards says when they have finished laughing. "Tell us another joke."

"Um, ok... What game does an alien love to play?" Harley says.

"I don't know," the alien guards reply. "What game does an alien love to play?"

"Astro-*nauts* and crosses."

"Hahahaha!" the guards laugh again. "Another one. Another one!"

"What's an alien's favorite key on a keyboard?"

"What? What?" the Trouserdown Guards ask eagerly.

"The space bar!"

"Hahahaha!" they both fall down again. They love Harley's jokes.

"What do aliens like to read?" Harley smiles.

"What?"

"*Comet* books!"

"Bahahahaha!"

What is wrong with those aliens? They must have a very unfunny planet if they find Harley's jokes funny.

I don't have long until Harley runs out of jokes. He can only keep them distracted for so long. I have to work fast.

While the Trouserdown Guards are lying on the ground laughing, I sneak behind the rocks towards the force-field generator machine.

This is my chance.

This is my opportunity to save Earth.

All I have to do is disable the force-field generator machine.

I reach the machine without being spotted by the alien guards. I swivel the side of it, and remove the panel to look at the controls.

Dad said I had to cut the red wire.

The red wire... the red wire... the red wire...

But I can't see a red wire?

Oh no!

What do I do now?!

"What are you doing?!" an alien guard shouts.

I look up and see one of the guards next to me.

Agh!

No!

This is not good!

I haven't turned off the force-field generator machine yet!

No!

WHACK!

The Trouserdown Guard thumps me with his arm, and I go flying across the meteor!

Ouch!

These guards are strong!

"Hey, you should leave me alone!" I say as he comes towards me again.

"Why?"

"Because I am just trying to fix your force-field generator machine," I try to trick the Trouserdown Guard. "It wasn't sending the right signals outward, so I am just trying to recalibrate the machine to function correctly with all the accurate dynamics. I'm really not trying to disable it so that I can steer the meteor away from Earth."

"Oh, ok," the Trouserdown Guard stands aside, and lets me go back to the machine. "You can go and fix our machine."

Yes!

I have tricked him!

Now, time to turn off the force-field generator...

WHACK!

Ouch!

The other Trouserdown Guard hits me!

"It's ok," the dumb one says to the other one. "He is just trying to fix the force-field generator machine. He really isn't trying to disable it so that he can steer the meteor away from Earth."

"No, he has tricked you!" the other Trouserdown Guard says. "He was going to disable it! We will have to punish him for his bad behavior!"

"Really?" the dumb one looks at me. "Were you trying to trick me by telling me a lie?"

"Noooo," I reply.

"See?" he says to the other Trouserdown Guard. "He wasn't trying to trick me. He was trying to fix it."

"No! He is tricking you again!" the Trouserdown Guard shouts. "Do not let him trick you!"

Uh-oh.

The Trouserdown Guards look angry.

Even for aliens, they look angry.

Yep, there is no mistaking that look on their faces. It is definitely anger.

Today isn't going the way I planned it.

I thought I would be sitting at home, pretending to study for my next math test while playing computer games.

Instead, I am on a meteor in space, about to be crushed by an alien that is wearing trousers around his ankles.

I definitely didn't predict that.

The Trouserdown Guard reaches down to grab me.

Oh no.

I'm doomed...

Chapter 8

Wrestling an Alien Guard

The Trouserdown Guard grips his hand around my arm.

Ouch!

His grip is so strong!

I struggle against his arm, but it is no use. He is too tough.

It's over.

I cannot defeat aliens this strong!

"Wait!"

It's Harley!

"If you crash this meteor into Earth, then I will never get to learn the Modularity Theorem! That is not acceptable, and I cannot let that happen!!" Harley shouts at the alien guards.

The alien guards look confused.

I doubt they have studied the Modularity Theorem.

"Oh, do you mean the theorem that states any elliptic curve over Q can be obtained via a rational map with integer coefficients from the classical modular curve $X_0(N)$ for integer N and is a curve with integer coefficients with an explicit definition?" the dumb one asks.

"Um, yes," Harley replies. "That is the theorem that I was talking about. How do you know that theorem?"

"I don't."

"But you just explained it?"

"Did I?" the guard looks at the other one. "Did I just explain that theorem?"

"I think so," the other one scratches his chin. "I can't remember now."

Oh, wow.

I would hate to be partnered up with these guys on a school project.

"If you blow up Earth, then you will *never* have any more trousers," Harley continues. "And that won't solve your problem of cold ankles! You'll have to live with cold ankles forever if you crash this meteor into Earth!"

"But if we can't have the trousers, then nobody can!" the alien guard argues. "We will not allow anyone else in the universe to have the trousers!"

"Yeah!" the other alien guard agrees. "If we cannot have the trousers, then we must destroy them all!"

As the Trouserdown Guards are distracted by Harley, I manage to slip free!

Yes!

Time to take the guards out!

"Hey, Trouserdown Guards! It's time to go home!" I yell as I ready my attack!

Then...

POW!

POW!

POW!

Yes!

I unload my best punch combo on the Trouserdown Guards!

Nobody would be able to withstand such a devastating attack!

Yes!

"Woo! We did it, Harley! We beat the aliens!" I start dancing in celebration of our awesome victory.

"Charlie," Harley tugs on my arm as I dance. "Charlie?"

"What?"

"I don't think you have defeated them."

I stop celebrating, and turn around to look at the Trouserdown Guards.

What?

The Trouserdown Guards are not lying on their backs – they are just standing still and looking at me!

"Did you feel that?" one of them asks the other.

"Nope. Didn't feel a thing," the other one says.

What?

How could someone resist my crazy combo!

"Charlie, I don't think they even felt that," Harley whispers to me. "You didn't even hurt them."

"Maybe they can resist my three punch combo attack," I stare at the Trouserdown Guards. "But they won't be able to resist my mega ninja strike attack!"

And...

POW! CRACK! STRIKE!

BANG! TICKLE! BANGY BANG!

HUG! POW! CUDDLE! BANG!

"Take that!" I puff at the end of my totally awesome attack combo.

Wow, that was hard work, but at least they are defeated now.

"Did you feel that combo?" the dumb Trouserdown Guard asks the other one.

"Um, nope. Still didn't feel a thing."

Aw, man.

They resisted my mega ninja strike attack combo!

They didn't feel anything!

"We don't feel pain," the Trouserdown Guard says. "We did not feel your punches."

Oh, come on!

They could have told me that before I wasted all of my energy trying to stop them!

"Charlie, what do we do now? You must have another plan, right? Right?" Harley hides behind me. "If you don't have a plan, we're wrecked, Charlie."

"We're not wrecked yet, Harley. We have to do something to stop them. My deadly combo attacks didn't stop them, but there must be something we can do," I say as I start to move back from the guards.

"It's time for us to destroy you," the Trouserdown Guards say.

No! What are we going do?!

I don't have another plan!

We're toast!

"But wait…" Harley tries to think of something else to say.

"Come on, Harley. Think of something really, really, really smart," I mumble as the Trouserdown Guards hover over us. "

"I've got it!" Harley shouts.

This had better be good.

If not, then this meteor is going to crash into Earth!

Chapter 9

A Math Problem!

The meteor seems to be getting faster as we continue to head towards Earth.

We cannot let this meteor crash into Earth! We must turn off the force-field generator machine, and turn this lump of rock around!

But first, we must defeat the Trouserdown Guards!

"Wait!" Harley stops the guards.

"No," they respond.

"Yes!" Harley yells back.

"No!"

"Yessy-yes!"

"Nooy-no!"

"Yessy-yessy-yes."

"Nooy-nooy-no!"

"Yessy-yessy-yessy-yes."

"Nooy-nooy-nooy-no!"

Hmmm. This could go on for a while.

"Stop it!" I stop the conversation from going any further. "Trouserdown Guards, you need to listen to what my friend Harley has to say. It is very important."

Whatever he has to say, I hope it is good.

"So Trouserdown Guards, what do you need the trousers for?" Harley asks.

"To keep our ankles warm."

"Is that all?"

"Yes."

"And how many aliens are on your planet?" Harley continues.

"We have 400 residents on our very, very cold planet. However, our bodies are very tough and the only place we feel the cold is on our ankles."

"Right. When Charlie's Super Spy Dad landed on your planet, he gave you 2000 pairs of trousers. What happened to those?"

"We have used them all. We wear the trousers every day, and they got old, so we had to throw them out."

"He also gave you 320,000 pairs of extra-extra large socks as a gift. What happened to the socks?"

"All those socks are still in their boxes. We don't know what to do with them. They are useless to us."

"The socks are for your ankles!" Harley shouts. "They are designed to keep your ankles warm! Look! I'm wearing astronaut socks now! They keep my ankles warm!"

"Ohhhh…" the alien guards say together. "We thought that the socks were for your ears. That didn't feel very comfortable. And we don't get cold ears, so we thought we didn't need them."

"But we don't have enough socks for everyone," the other Trouserdown Guard says. "We would run out of socks too quickly."

"You have enough socks for everyone!" Harley states.

"No, we don't. Everyone needs at least ten pairs of socks each. With 320,000 socks and 400 aliens, that's… um… um… um…"

"You have 320,000 pairs of socks and 400 aliens... 320,000 divided by 400..." Harley does the math in his head. "That means you have 800 pairs of socks each!"

"800 pairs of ankle warming socks each?!" the alien guards ask in surprise. "So our ankles wouldn't get cold?"

"Yes!"

"Ohhhhh..... That's way more than we need!" they laugh together. "Ok. Well, don't worry about the email."

"And sorry about threatening to blow up your planet, and all that!" the other alien guard laughs.

The Trouserdown Guards slowly turn around and walk over to the force-field machine. They turn it off and hand the machine to me as a souvenir.

"Sorry!" the alien guards say again.

"We'll turn the meteor around, and fly back to our planet to tell everyone how to use the socks. They will be so surprised! That is so clever! Who would have thought that socks went on your feet?! So clever!"

"Yeah!" the other alien guard laughs. "We don't even need the trousers any more!"

"Wait…" the biggest alien guard stops.

"What's wrong?" I ask.

"We are the Trouserdown Guards. We can't be the Trouserdown Guards without trousers."

"You can be the Extra-Extra Large Sock Guards," I suggest.

"Yeah!" the alien guards laugh again, and begin to program the meteor to turn around using their own steering control panel. "You should leave in your spaceship. We will fly this meteor back to our planet, and start to use the extra-extra large socks. Bye!"

"Ok," I smile. "Bye!"

Chapter 10

Going Home

"Wow Harley," I say as I look at my friend. "You are so awesome!"

Harley smiles proudly as we walk back to our spaceship.

"We did it," he says. "We stopped the meteor crashing into Earth! I didn't think that we would be able to do it, but we did it!"

"It's amazing what you can achieve when you just try," I smile.

Once we have launched our spaceship and start to fly back to Earth, the meteor turns around. It is no longer going to destroy Earth.

"Dad," I call Super Spy headquarters on the Intergalactic Communicator. "We have done it! Harley convinced the Trouserdown Guards, I mean the Extra-Extra Large Sock Guards, to turn the meteor around and go home."

"Great news, Charlie!" Dad celebrates. "Well done, Harley! I am very proud of you boys! Great job!"

"We will be back on Earth within the hour," I report.

"Good. Remember to press all the right button combinations for a safe landing," Dad says.

"Um, yep. No problem. No problem at all…" I reply. "We will see you soon."

I hang up the Intergalactic Communicator and look at Harley, who is smiling happily as he gazes at Earth in the distance.

"Mrs. Jackson was right," I say as we fly through space.

"How?" Harley smiles.

"Math is useful!" I laugh. "Math actually saved the day!"

"True!" Harley laughs. "We just saved the world using math!"

All in a day's work for a Super Spy, I guess...

The End

Also in the Diary of a Super Spy series:

Diary of a Super Spy

Diary of a Super Spy: Attack of the Ninjas!

Diary of a Super Spy: A Giant Problem!

Diary of a Super Spy: Evil Attack!

Diary of a Super Spy: Daylight Robbery!

Also by Peter Patrick and William Thomas:

Diary of a Ninja Spy

Diary of a Ninja Spy 2

Diary of a Ninja Spy 3

Diary of a Ninja Spy 4

Diary of a Time Spy

From the Authors

Thank you for reading 'Diary of a Super Spy: Space!'

Like all students in 6th Grade, Charlie Chucky is learning that life's adventures are so much more enjoyable when they are shared with friends.

We hope you will join Charlie on his next journey – 'Diary of a Super Spy: Evil Attack!'

Have fun!

Peter Patrick and William Thomas

If you liked this story, please leave a review!

Special Preview Chapter:

Diary of a Super Spy:

Evil Attack!

Peter Patrick

William Thomas

Chapter 1

Monday

Monday is supposed to be a fun day.

Supposed to be.

But not this Monday. No way. Uh-uh. Nope. There is nothing fun about this Monday. Nothing at all.

Today, my class is in the gym playing dodge-ball.

I'm not very good at dodge-ball because:

a) I'm not very good at dodging balls,

b) I'm not very good at throwing balls and;

c) I'm not very good at any sports.

Oh man...

My name is Charlie Chucky, I am in the sixth grade, I love playing Minecraft, and I am learning to become a Super Spy.

My Dad is the world's best Super Spy, and he is starting to teach me all his awesome tricks. Lately, I've been battling invisible monsters, crazy zombie teachers, and super ninjas!

Life has been pretty crazy, but I've enjoyed every second of it.

But as awesome as life is outside of school hours, it still doesn't save me from the terrors of the sixth grade. I still have to deal with girls, really smelly teachers, and bullies.

Big Cooper Stanley is our school's resident bully.

Last week, he made every boy in school hand over their lunch.

And then he gave it all back. He just likes to take things.

Big Cooper Stanley likes to call me 'Tea Party Charlie.' He has said it 5000 times, but he still laughs every time he says it.

I've never even played tea parties, but somehow that's the name that he has invented for me.

This is Cooper.

Today, Cooper seems more evil than normal.

He has already tripped over four teachers, pulled down the trousers of two students, and splashed water over three people.

And it's not even lunchtime yet!

That's a massively crazy rate of bullying – even for Cooper.

Something has changed in Cooper. He seems bigger, angrier, and even nastier.

I wonder why he is even meaner than usual...

Read the rest of the adventure in:

Diary of a Super Spy:

Evil Attack!

Available to buy now!